Past That, Still There

poems by

Geoffrey Godbey

Finishing Line Press
Georgetown, Kentucky

Past That, Still There

ACKNOWLEDGMENTS

Some of these poems appeared previously in *The World and I, Pivot, The Little Magazine, Town and Gown, Twelve Festival Poets* and *Quest*.

Publisher: Leah Maines

Editor: Christen Kincaid

Cover Art: Driving Through A Dream by Barbara Metzner (barbarametzner.com)

Author Photo: Ken Noel Photography, State College, PA

Cover Design: Elizabeth Maines McCleavy

Printed in the USA on acid-free paper.
Order online: www.finishinglinepress.com
            also available on amazon.com

Author inquiries and mail orders:
Finishing Line Press
P. O. Box 1626
Georgetown, Kentucky 40324
U. S. A.

Table of Contents

To Barbara

ALONG FOR THE RIDE

I have become the
Director of Trees,
Superintendent of the Sky.

I have become harmless;
a lot for a man.

I have become happy;
the futures market
for self-pity
down based on evidence.

The wind has promised
no more mischief
from its old urge.

Folks who love me.

Numb sequence
of life that
runs so well
without us.

Without me.

Driving through a dream.

Along for the ride.

What a dream.

What a ride.

What a big fat
lost long ride.

THERE ARE TIMES

1.
There are times
when it is clear.

The bare-branched trees
an explosion,
a eureka,
a sudden prayer.

No need for
a recipient
to come forward.

There is
the frozen earth
which forgets its
green days.

There are deer
jumping out
of the void,
appearing from
some dream
I could not
construct
on my own.

On my own
how far
could I get
in the winter
of wanting?
What in me
could run?

2.
What runs
the frozen field
runs my heart.

Arced wing of cloud
numb but
needing nothing

gliding with
our ancestors
contained within.

Waiting to touch
the ever
slowly coming.

PLAYGROUND BASKETBALL

They move
up and down court
like star-eyed horses

clump together
as if awaiting a meteor

squeak at the feet

hurry to their secret spots
sea-splashed and glistening
like fish that jump
out of the ocean.

Black men with
a broken moon . . .

One small hole
in the sky.

AGNOSTIC PRAYER

Make me a seed
dry and dead
in a paper envelope

idle in darkness
but sensing
the blooming to come.

There will be water.

Vine and flower.

Then a happy
dying back
from inexplicable life.

Blind in
the envelope.

Blind in the ground.

Beginning to see
as the sun
remembers us.

Seeing the sky
as heaven.

Crawling and climbing
toward fullness.

Make me a seed.

DRIVING TO THE GYM

Driving through
the little village
early on a
January morning
the dark mountain ahead
is a wave
frozen to the earth
which has no need
to reach the shore.

My I phone sits face up
staring at the ceiling
of the car
all its tricks
easily awakened
and the car moves
so certainly
generating
some of its energy
from its own movement.

May I be like the car.

May I be like the phone.

But most of all
may I be
like the mountain.

MARCH

March sees
the possibilities:
an old man
turning at last
toward love.

The wind
returns
to itself
and tells her

faith, old child,
what loves you
will arrive.

The ground
still cold
as the dead
but stirring.

Lion and lamb;
dreams whistling
the heart's song
in the wind.

It is coming
and there is
still time.

LIGHT

1.
There are times
in December
when sun
leaves the ridge
as if to remind us . . .

my gray breath
aches

blows cold as
the last tally
of steps
toward grace
we have
yet to take.

2.
Paintings in
the little gallery
across the road
show that light
is mostly imagined

old women
stand with brushes
finding ways to let
the late light
of their lives
do what cannot
be done solely
by intention
but also by
the gift
of imagined
light.

STAIRS IN CHINA

They love stairs
guessing
where they go.
Rising by
their own agility
against the odds.

The stairs
have no hand rails,
risers uneven
but they go up mountains,
move toward fat Buddhas,
golden and ignorant
in the afternoon's
smoky sun.

They think
they can climb
into the sky
even though
the women wear
impossible shoes.

They dream of stairs
that could
finally take them
where they need
to go.

It is never the same
going down
the stairs,

the only time
you can fall.

TELL ME

There are things
you could tell me
I could tell you
if we first admit
we are crazy,
watching a crazy world
not knowing
if the important thing
is bombs or bunnies
doing their stare off
and sky hop
in the far field
at evening.

There are things
we might share.

What makes
awkward sense
to you?

What lifts that impulse
lost in your gizzard,
floats your blue boat
and to where?

There are things
we could say
or maybe
be comfortable
with silence . . .

respecting what
it tells.

AMERICAN IDOL

God enters American Idol
comes in third
the finalists a shrill
singing woman
with most of
her clothes off
and a hip hop guy
who loves the world
but thinks
he is the world.

The judges tell God
he has talent
but needs to
speed things up,
six days and all,
and also
lose the beard.

SONG

You might not hear my song begin.
It's melody sounds quite like the wind.

Its rhythm which continues till morning
is seven drunks in a hotel snoring.

The first verse deals with all the specifics
of my life by means of hieroglyphics.

The last verse is a complete collection
of the itemized costs of resurrection.

All the lyrics in between
speak on ends but never means.

The lyrics can be sung or spoke.
They climb the air like hardwood smoke.

TRUMP

The lice have leaped
toward cheaper flesh

a rat is drunk
on the harp strings

the mockingbird
has flown into the thorns

and I am asleep
in the barrel of their gun.

WHAT

What tells you?
What speaks?
What makes the point
that will not let you sleep?

What shows you
without effort or intent?
What simply lives alongside,
is never adamant?

What casts its spell,
forever holds you?
What touches so subtly
its presence presupposed you?

What gives with no taking?
Lives without waking?
What thrives in your life's dream?
What is but need not seem?

SNOW-BLIND

Today the blind
stare holes
though blindness.
The rest are dazed
by snow.

Last night I heard
a trumpet
that plays
all its lifetime.

This morning,
in a snowy corner,
sorrow's game was
solitaire.

At last we leap
from our
secret places
and follow
the bodiless wings
without question.

THE WIND IN WINTER

1.
The wind has come.

An ocean
in the mind
of an honest man.

A fever which
knocks and rolls
among the
heathen trees.

A light for those
who no longer
open their eyes.

2.
I am well
toward sleep,
which is the
wind's father.

I will dream
all night of the
lost mother
of the wind.

ROMANCE

Night wind
in the tall trees.

The trees think
they have
somewhere
 to go.

The wind thinks
it has
somewhere
to stay.

RIVER

Like the wind
except for
its belonging
never asking
where
sun glint
on flying beads
which re-join
downstream
so many creeks
feed it
children
joining parents
and it moves
as one
as later
we must move
broken and sparkling
and never
ask where.

LIMERICKS

A man named P. Lewis Pews
kept hamsters in his shoes.
In his shirt there were rats.
In his top hat five bats
but his wife and kids were in zoos.

A dirty old woman named Ross
was addicted to Worcestershire sauce.
Though she could not renounce it
or even pronounce it
whatever she ate tasted boss.

A troll who lived under a bridge
decided to move to a ridge.
He was no longer wet
and how easy to get
frozen billy-goats out of the frig.

Overworked old Santa Claus
cried: "Everything is lost.
While flying quite high
in the sulphuric sky
I ran into a damned albatross."

A hamster who bulked up on roids
with a high-tech army of droids
took over the Senate
but within a minute
the droids were annoyed by the void.

A man who talked for FOX news
had his brains concealed in his shoes.
He was able to talk
and able to walk
but the truth left his shoes without clues.

Said Fitztipton Beauregard Biddle
"Your verse is inclined to piddle.
I'm already quite sick
from these limericks
let us end them right here in the middle."

SUPPOSE

the dead
wish to speak
to us
and
the language
they have
is the moon.

NOW THAT WE KNOW EVERYTHING

Distances are
the same
but the paths
are numbered.

There is a crack
in the night
through which
we see
another night.

We find that
the language of trees
is silence.

God's season
of reruns
at last begins.

LETTING GO

For RB

It is not, as has been observed, the fall that kills you. It is the landing. Pears on trees let go. Glue bonding two pieces of wood suddenly becomes weary and snaps. The hand that holds relaxes and what it thought it owned flies away. Ice on a car roof clings as long as it can then cracks and flies back into a history which cannot be read. And the driver feels some lightness and loss.

Geese are high over you--and at first you think they are going and you have stayed but then the twilight begins dreaming and it is dark and nothing has gone or stayed.

Letting go happens when you say, after some lesson of living "I am back to square one" but there are no squares. The door is opened and someone says "hello" to emptiness, and enters, clouds framed in a window, on that journey which is always from the known to the unknown. Clouds revealing the blue void within their phosphorescence. Clouds shining as they let go, dancing without effort or purpose, their last light drained by the disinterested sun, which is late for its next appointment. In such splendid suspension rise the quick empires of ever, where we live as singular beings in all our beauty and strangeness.

You cannot really speak of this. Rescue is futile since there is nothing to rescue you for or from. You have let go and are being carried. Indians knew this. The simple people who danced and ate and thought themselves unimportant--except in their letting go-- knew this. And we learn.

You let go because you can, the old longing still in you, swimming toward the endless, which you will not understand--and it is finally wonderful in its mystery. The answers each fail, having bought only time or made money or given power or pushed a problem back a few years or miles. The answers in their bravery were like our hands which hold what enters and pretend to know it. They carried you a long way but still it got dark. In that darkness you raised your hands to feel your way and touched a face you have always known.

It is enough. The trees know what to do without us. The sky has its plan. The great night is content. Tires sing on the highway of our folly.

There is nothing left but who you are and who you are sits across the aisle from you on a plane and then there is no plane, leaving you in the rare air beside yourself and miles past fear and answers.

When you let go it seems you are falling backward but everything, instead, is moving away from you and you recall as a child how it seemed the train you were on was not moving but the scenery was.

And you move away from the clock at the speed of light so the clock stays forever at 12 and in that eternal instant you have let go and there is more strength in the "letting" than in the "going."

And the letting is not the leaving for there is no longer anything to leave or return to and the dead dog buried in your ground is near you and knows something important has happened.

OTHER WAYS

There are other ways
arriving in the dark
through the branches
of familiar trees
and they are often
too late
but still
they are there

and these
other ways
roll across the bed
as you twist
toward the next
insufficient sleep
gliding into your
consciousness
as you watch the
black strip of cloud
try to hide the moon

but the moon remains
like these
other ways
that bypass you
and speak directly
to your life.

SOMETIMES

a signal
that has
bound around
the universe
like a forgotten ancestor
finds you after
everything seems
to have happened
waking you suddenly
from your sleep
and requesting a name

one name

and that name
which you will
call out from instinct
even against
your understanding
will be who was meant
by the mountains
and deep water
for your life
to fill your emptiness
which was like
sunglasses
on a blind man.

You obey and
there is nothing else
nor need be
and the birds fly
in your honor
and the stars
for one night
change their path
and make you

their promise
as you
make them yours.

A PHASE

I live my
life of doors
within an amber
inch of sleep.

The pale light
gains and loses
on my green rug
like a wave.

I meet myself
coming and going;
only my
privacy's saved.

I'd beat it down
if words I chose
could hold the things
I'd have them keep.

I live my life of doors
within an amber
inch of sleep.

THE RAINMAKER

If rain had passengers
I would be one.

If piles of leaves
took in boarders
I would stay
among them,
happy to be lost.

If the night
introduced itself
we might find
we had
friends in common.

If my poem did
as I wished
it would fall
back upon me
like rain.

LEARNING TO SLEEP ON YOUR SIDE

It is the arms that
no longer know
what to do.

When you used to
fly into the bed
on your stomach
or rise toward heaven
on your back
the arms knew
their place

but now one arm
feels rolled on
by a suddenly
uncaring body
and the other hangs
from the top shoulder
in fear of falling
off the hip.

So as sleep
finally finds you
the arms reunite,
top arm
extending its hand
to the elbow
of the bottom arm
and they begin
the process
that lets us curl
into ourselves.

A process that
goes on and on.

CAMERA

1.
I never much liked cameras
preferring to see who I am
in clear water,
the rest through my eyes.

But there were always
cameras to rob the now.
Closer, a little closer,
say cheese and
the moment was gone.

2.
Do not stop tourists
with your camera.
Let them capture
the moment later
if it remembers
the way back to them.

Anything you freeze
is changed.
My mother was always
uncomfortable when
the camera saw her,
could not pretend
its absence
and it reduced her
to an old lady
addled,
wanting to please,
not knowing how.

3.
I get photos
from trips
to China or Brazil

people say
there we were
it was wonderful
but I still trust
pictures
the heart saves
that have carried me
all the way to here
more than a camera.

GEEZER

It is the time
when your life
learns to fly
without you

and you
a mourning dove
with that slight stall
between the event
and flight
getting longer

new things
requesting your worry

so many you love
did not understand
it could not be
the same
after the years
remembered their name
made their claim
on the past
like water scooped
into cupped hands

children giving their
crayon love
as we become clouds
moving toward the edge
of some screen
we did not want
to have turned on.

A TRUCK ON THE TURNPIKE

The eighteen-wheeler
goes by
making the sound
of heavy loss
and each
small orange light
on its cab
says to the
darkness:

Forgive me.

Go back to sleep.

This is not
my doing.

LOVE POEM WRITTEN AGAINST LOVE POEMS

Oh, the holes in your ears!
Cilia in your nose tipped with soot
and waving like wheat in a dust storm.
The creased skin where your arm has bent
a million times and not fallen off.
Half-moons of your toenails
rising silently through your sandals.
Your eyebrows' dandruff.
The way it looks naked behind your ears.
Small webs of skin between your fingers;
crosshatched and ghostly.
The blue veins of your wrists
leading off into underground rivers
and the ugliness of the back of your tongue
living damp and discreetly
within your sweet darkness.

These are the parts
for the long haul, Babe.

A WINTER EVENING

Orange dance
down a black mouth
far off in the west.

Snow fills in
my footprints
behind me.

Snow stays on
into sleep
like some aspiration
never there
upon waking.

FORGETTING

When the November wind
blows through its stone teeth
portable barbecues go into hiding.

Drivers scrape frost from windshields
expecting to find a frozen body
behind the wheel.

Black flies in the closet
are stiff and dizzy
like spots before the eyes.

Old lovers flicker
At the bottom of
laundry hampers,
their amber faces
out of focus.

The cold night
becomes too clear
to live in.

TOURIST

There are places
you can go
but when you arrive
someone walks out
from a broken spot
and says
this is really nowhere
the place
you were looking for
was eaten by a small dog-
eaten to sustain himself
and the empire
erected in its place
leaked on the original
like an old man
with a prostate problem

so if you can
just find out how
to return to your
last place and life
you will hear the song
you have always
wanted to sing
being sung by rabbits
trees waving in time
to the music
and your bed,
which was no longer
a bed without you,
finds its former duty
is now your greatest joy.

NO MORE BOOKS

The time came
when there was
no more
ink on paper
only bits of electricity
appearing in the
unthought-of instant
and we
reduced our footprints,
then our feet,
then our need to eat,
then breathe
like so many ghosts
becoming holy
to whom, to whom?

NOT THE FIRST TIME

It is not the first time
I have been
instructed by the morning
thin air
clouds coming to life
and the sun
making the same decision
which is our lives
and I have never known
what response
there could be to this
the day thinking
it is the first
and the branches waving
to whomever
and people
hidden in cars
flying about
to things that
seem to
require their presence
and the empty blue sky
which goes up
as far as your imagination
will allow it.

NEW MATH

1.
The great nothing
we have added up to

new math same as the old.

Ignoring dreaming stars.

The willow's wanting.

A perfect question
from the imperfect child.

Small celebration of raspberries.

Ignoring the grasshopper
whose green motor
hums in its
elusive world

Ignoring the
numb moon's
majesty

while we saw
the legs
off our
left over soldiers.

2.
We are
the long-talking deaf

blind parachutists
drowning
in the singing water
pushing

heaven's button
inside the
burning elevator.

3.
Ho Chi Minh stirs.

The phantom boat
goes on alone.

Hills left shivering
from understanding.

In tighter circles
the turkey vulture glides
closer to the ground.

The numbers of
the dead
called like a
bingo game

and it adds up
new math—old math
to nothing.

GRINDSTONE

Keeping your nose to
the grindstone
produces a very small nose
which cannot smell basil,
or moist morning air

and when you finally
look up
there are animals
that can fly
and strange things
shooting out of the ground
in the most delicious
shapes and colors
water dripping
making rhythm and melody

some ancient song
you have
finally heard
and you want to tell
all this to someone
but they have gone
leaving a trail

but you can
no longer
smell their scent.

THE WINTER OF 94

Last night it got so cold
the trees asked to come inside.

Stars huddled together
creating a second moon.

Even living in the furnace
you needed a sweater.

Smoke from the
sore throats
of chimneys
crystallized in the air
and peppered the roofs.

TV pictures froze in place.

In earmuffs, musicians
endlessly played the same note.

Snowflakes shattered upon arrival.

Mannequins sneezed in store windows.

Night froze to the ground
like a stuck garage door
and when it was finally melted
by thousands of back yard fires

all we got was the anorexic sun
just to the north of everywhere.

THE RIDDLE, THE PRAYER

Father of leaves and long clocks
the road repairs itself in circles
but the walls end one by one.

Drop roots and the road roams.
Barricade it; the landscape swirls.
I have hired a pumpkin to teach me to dance.
Looking for tracks I have found my feet.

Mother of deep roots and dark roads
I live in response to a forgotten question.

TRYING TO EXPLAIN

Yes. Yes. No.
I don't know.
I think. I guess.
Your fleeting face
along the boulevard.
The sun like
a hot rock
flung west.

I know three ways
to answer
what we
never guessed.
Your thin hands reach
but cannot hold.
They dream
but will not rest.

My large hands
hold what enters.
Lost between
lilac dreams
and the practical
cars of Japan,
my hands consider
empty extremes.

DOUBTS FOR A COLD JUNE DAY

1.
A special sorrow
gropes among the trees
like a single hand.

The rope bridge between
waking and sleeping
breaks one strand at a time.

2.
Today I need names
for my misunderstandings
or a night
in green language.

Today I need
the sleepwalking ants
whose feet never doubt
their love for the earth.

Today I need
a voice that
has come here
in the same steady light.

The only way
on the only road.

Let it speak to
the rumor of my life.

THE REPAIRMAN

At last he comes
with tools and light;
clear-eyed and ugly.

His hushed hands move
and we wait . . .

No cure, he says, no cure
but the pipes and pistons
pledge us another year
and the unfixable silence
still plays its music
beyond our mornings.

LEAST

It is that
least bit of voice
you hear when
coming out of
whatever sleep
found you.
A shard of voice
from someone
who once told you
their feelings
like a waterfall
cleansing you in rain
but now
must hint
in your
twilight conscious
because their voice
is ghost
and you are not yet
but hearing the voice
you are another step
toward living in
that other world
of air

where so many
spend forever
choosing the small phrase
they can speak
to the sleepers
yet living.

PAST THAT, STILL THERE

1.
Whatever has quit asking.
Whatever does not nod
to the wind.

Rhythms
of politics
razor blades
hitting a drum

and backlit screens
we thought
were our lives. . .

I am past all that.

Cars which move
themselves
burning one percent
for us.

Ground bodies
of cows
we never knew.

Past the thought
we are free as spiders
up a chosen wall.

Past know-nothing heroes
who cannot bow
to the coming era
of suffering.

Past the proposition
we know how
our heads

got screwed on
the bulge
we do not own
the wisdom
fat and glistening
riding our ignorant lives
magic jockey
deep in slumber
on a horse
lost in pleasure.

2.
But I am still there
for mysterious trees
which wave at both
past and future

the child from China
dancing with life
in her pretty dress
and unceasing questions

For the sugar maple
which has weak wood
from too much
sweet emotion

I am there.

And for the legions
of silent women
wanting nothing more
than their place
in the ages.

The slow-motion dance
of the sky.

The family
one discovers
in old age.

And the love
that requires
everything
but effort

I am there.

Still there.

LONE DOG

Lone dog of memory
white road
no master
but some old longing.

Evening slowly
coming to its senses.

A first yellow star
in the dark blue heaven

happy without trying.

Born in Lexington, Kentucky, **Geoffrey Godbey** has lived many places in the Northeastern United States and Canada. His parents read poetry to him when he was a child and he came to love words, as did his father, seeing a way in them. His early writing was influenced by Robert Bly and, later, by W.S. Merwin. John Haag and Joseph Grucci taught him and US Poet Laureate Donald Hall tried to get a manuscript of his published. An early chapbook—*The Midget On A Bicycle*—was published by Mansfield Press. His poetry has also appeared in *The Nation, The World and I,* and many literary magazines. Godbey was a Festival Poet for the Central Pennsylvania Festival of the Arts. His poetry has also appeared in textbooks for public school students. Finishing Line Press published *Finding Home* in 2013.

His roles in life have been diverse. Born legally blind, his vision got better. He has been a dancer on American Bandstand, a playground leader, a young husband and father of two daughters, a Viet Nam war protestor, professional drummer, tennis instructor, a Professor at the University of Waterloo in Canada and Penn State University, and an international traveller. His books on leisure, tourism and parks and recreation have sold over 100,000 copies. China has been a special interest in later life and he has visited the country more than a dozen times. A vegetarian for more than three decades, he is an avid vegetable gardener. The publishing company he co-founded, Venture Publishing, has been in business for 34 years. Godbey lives on a ridge in State College Pennsylvania and shares life with his partner the artist Barbara Metzner.

www.ingramcontent.com/pod-product-compliance
Lightning Source LLC
Chambersburg PA
CBHW021204090426
42740CB00008B/1222